MERCY

THE DIVINE RESCUE OF THE HUMAN RACE

JESUS IS LORD®

KENNETH COPELAND
PUBLICATIONS

Mercy—The Divine Rescue of the Human Race
Formerly titled: *The Mercy of God*

ISBN-10 0-88114-725-7   30-0024
ISBN-13 978-0-88114-725-4

25 24 23 22 21 20   21 20 19 18 17 16

© 1986 Eagle Mountain International Church Inc. aka Kenneth Copeland Ministries

Kenneth Copeland Publications
Fort Worth, TX 76192-0001

For more information about Kenneth Copeland Ministries, visit kcm.org or call 1-800-600-7395 (U.S. only) or +1-817-852-6000.

CONTENTS

ONE

THE *Nature* OF GOD

S ince the Garden of Eden, God has had to deal with man at arm's length because of the glory surrounding His being. It would overwhelm man if God appeared to him in the full manifestation of His power. He once revealed to Moses that no man could look into His face and live and then only allowed him a glimpse of Himself from behind. He said, "I will put you in the shadow and cleft of a rock. I will hold My hand over your face as I allow My goodness to pass before you." (See Exodus 33:19-23.)

Mercifully, God protected Moses from

the intense power that radiated from His face, knowing that even the shadow of His presence would be too much for him.

However, this distance between man and Himself was not in God's original plan. He had created Adam and clothed him in His own light and glory. Adam did not know he was naked.

Before Adam sinned, all he knew was the fire of God's glory around his body. However, after the Fall of Man, Adam lost that fire and could no longer fellowship with God in His presence as he had before. If he had, the glory of God which consumes all sin would have consumed him as well.

God wanted to restore our relationship with Him so He could walk and talk with us like He did with Adam. His desire is to have fellowship with us. He sent Jesus to the earth to pay the price for man's sin. Through Jesus, the glory of God came wrapped in human flesh so that once again man and his Creator could have contact.

GOD WANTS TO WALK AND TALK WITH US LIKE HE DID WITH ADAM.

Jesus was born of a virgin, without sin. The Holy Spirit hovered over Mary and there was conceived in her a holy thing (Luke 1:35). Jesus was born not of a natural man, but God Himself caused life to come into Mary's womb.

God's life flowed into His human body.

The glory of God did not consume Jesus as it would a sinful man. Instead, it became a flowing stream of healing that radiated from the person of Jesus. A vivid illustration of this is the account of Jesus on the Mount of Transfiguration, when His clothes and face literally shone with the glory of God.

Today, we are no longer restricted from the presence of God's glory. The New Covenant tells us very plainly that the God who shined out of darkness has "shined in our hearts, to give [us] the light of the knowledge of the glory of God in the face of Jesus Christ" (2 Corinthians 4:6-7). God put His glory in us because His mercy endures forever. His mercy was greater than all the sin in the whole world.

When Jesus, God's Son said, "Let this cup pass from Me" (Matthew 26:39), the Father could have done so. God could have said, "I will not bring all the sin of fallen humanity on the One righteous person who has walked the earth since the Garden of Eden." However, His mercy and enduring compassion was greater than what was about to happen to His Son.

Mercy overcame.

Jesus followed the example of His Father. He was always moved and led by compassion. He never acted on His own motives and ideas. Compassion and mercy dictated to His mind even when His body was suffering. It welled up within Him and produced joy—the joy that caused Him to endure the cross, despising the shame (Hebrews 12:2).

Tender COMPASSION

Jesus experienced the same compassion that causes a mother or a father to overcome the fear of personal harm for the sake of their child. A father will take on all the forces of hell and wade into odds far greater than himself when his family is threatened. His mercy and compassion is far greater than any danger he sees with his eyes and hears with his ears.

I will never forget one time when my daughter Kellie came and sat down on my lap. She was only 3 years old. I was looking at something else when she placed her two index fingers, one on each of my cheeks, and turned my face toward hers, which was right up in mine. As she pulled me closer she said, "Daddy, I love you." At that moment in time, if I owned the moon, I would have given it to her!

God will respond to His children when they express their love for Him, just as naturally as a parent will respond to his child who says, "I love you." The Word says that we get the similarity of our parenthood from God. Our role as parents is a model of the relationship we have with our heavenly Father.

We are never going to get anywhere shaking our fists in God's face. But when we get before Him and say, "I love You, You are the King of my life, and I will go anywhere You tell me to go, and do anything You tell me to do," God will respond to us compassionately.

When we take our place as His children, He will always take His place as our Father. God Almighty is the biggest love pushover in the whole world. He is fully aware of our every sin. He sent Jesus to the cross rather than condemn us, and He hasn't changed. He is still looking for opportunities to show His mercy.

In 2 Chronicles 5, He directed the children of Israel to put singers out in front of the army. They sang, "God is good. His mercy endureth forever." They were really saying to the enemy, "God loves us anyhow

> WHEN WE TAKE OUR PLACE AS HIS CHILDREN, HE WILL ALWAYS TAKE HIS PLACE AS OUR FATHER.

and you had better keep your hands off us!" In response, God moved on the enemy army before the Israelites got to them because they declared His mercy.

Notice also, that when the children of Israel began to shout about God's mercy, the place where they were gathered filled up with the glory of God. The presence of God was so powerful that the priests could not stand on their feet to minister. Verses 13-14 say:

> It came even to pass, as the trumpeters and singers were as one, to make one sound to be heard in praising and thanking the Lord; and when they lifted up their voice with the trumpets and cymbals and instruments of music, and praised the Lord, saying, For he is good; for his mercy endureth for ever: that then the house was filled with a cloud, even the house of the Lord; so that the priests could not stand to minister by reason of the cloud: for the glory of the Lord had filled the house of God.

Reason FOR WORSHIP

Mercy is the reason we worship God. It motivates us to walk holy before Him and gives us confidence that we can come before Him without fear. We can rest in knowing that the mercy of God is greater and stronger than anything else. It has unlimited endurance. Psalm 136 declares this:

O give thanks unto the Lord; for he is good: for his mercy endureth for ever. O give thanks unto the God of gods: for his mercy endureth for ever. O give thanks to the Lord of lords: for his mercy endureth for ever. To him who alone doeth great wonders: for his mercy endureth for ever. To him that by wisdom made the heavens: for his mercy endureth for ever. To him that stretched out the earth above the waters: for his mercy endureth for ever. To him that made great lights: for his mercy endureth for ever: the sun to rule by day: for his mercy endureth for ever: the moon and stars to rule by night: for his mercy endureth for ever. To him that smote Egypt in their firstborn: for his mercy endureth for ever: and brought out Israel from among them: for his mercy endureth for ever: with a strong hand, and with a stretched out arm: for his mercy endureth for ever. To him which divided the Red sea into parts: for his mercy endureth for ever: and made Israel to pass through the midst of it: for his mercy endureth for ever: but overthrew Pharaoh and his host in the Red sea: for his mercy endureth for ever. To him which led his people through the wilderness: for his mercy endureth for ever. To him which smote great kings: for his mercy endureth for ever: and slew famous kings: for his mercy endureth for ever: Sihon king of the Amorites: for his mercy endureth for ever: and Og the king of Bashan: for his mercy endureth for ever: and gave their land for an heritage: for his mercy endureth for ever: even an heritage unto Israel his servant: for his mercy endureth for ever: who remembered us in our low estate: for his mercy endureth for ever: and hath redeemed us from our enemies: for his mercy endureth for ever. Who giveth food to all flesh: for his mercy endureth for ever. O give thanks unto the God of heaven: for his mercy endureth for ever.

Looking at this you can see that each work of God is

covered by His mercy. And, among the things that the mercy of God put into operation are wonders, wisdom and His creative power.

Basis of GOD'S HOLINESS

God's mercy is great. Not only does it last forever, but it is holy. This is true because love, the source of mercy and compassion, is the basis of holiness. Every time we remember how holy God is, we are to give thanks and praise because "His mercy endureth forever."

Psalm 30:4-5 says: "Sing unto the Lord, O ye saints of his, and give thanks at the remembrance of his holiness. For his anger endureth but a moment; in his favour is life: weeping may endure for a night, but joy cometh in the morning."

Understand that although God, in being holy, sets up a standard against sin, it is not to prevent us from having a good time. Mercy is the motivating factor. God wants us to experience His joy by living and walking after His example. In His mercy, He is trying to keep us from sin which has the power to kill us. We are to rejoice in the protective mercy He has for us and worship Him because His holiness is an expression of His love. First Chronicles 16:25-33 instructs us to worship the Lord "in the beauty of holiness." It says:

> For great is the Lord, and greatly to be praised: he also is to be feared above all gods. For all the gods of the people are idols: but the Lord made the heavens. Glory and honour are in his presence; strength and gladness are in his place. Give unto the Lord, ye kindreds of the people, give unto the Lord glory and strength. Give unto the Lord the glory due unto his name: bring an offering, and come before him: worship the Lord in the beauty of holiness. Fear before him, all the earth: the world also shall be stable, that it be not moved. Let the heavens be glad, and let the earth rejoice: and let men say among the nations, The Lord reigneth. Let the sea roar, and the fulness thereof: let the fields rejoice, and all that is therein. Then shall the trees of the wood sing out at the presence of the Lord, because he cometh to judge the earth.

TWO

Greater THAN GOD'S WRATH

As you begin to analyze God's merciful nature, you will begin to understand the way He thinks. You will begin to gain new insights into the Word of God where you had no understanding before. I let myself be robbed of the first five years of my ministry because I did not understand God's mercy. Don't let that happen to you.

Don't allow condemnation to keep you from acting on the mercy of God. Follow what the Word says concerning it. Keep in mind that God's mercy is far greater than His wrath. Psalm 30:5 says, "For his anger endureth but a moment." By contrast, remember Psalm 136. His mercy endures forever.

God has always loved you. He loved you when you were a sinner and did not know Him. He loves the person who has violated every commandment there is. Because God's love is constant and He never changes, there is not anything you can do to make Him love you any more or any less. He loves you with all that He is—and He is love. Psalm 145:8-9 says: "The Lord is gracious, and full of compassion; slow to anger, and of great mercy. The Lord is good to all: and his tender mercies are over all his works." We do things that cause Him to have no pleasure in us, but He still loves us.

FROM SIN

We are secure in knowing that we can never change how much He loves us. Everything God does and all His thoughts are based on His mercy. These are the high thoughts and ways of Isaiah 55:8-9. His mercy is "over all his works." When we make mistakes, He looks tenderly at us with compassion.

The cry of God's heart is for us to run from all sin and

come to Him. He offers us a place of rest. He is continually saying, "Don't do that anymore. Come unto me, all ye that labour and are heavy laden, and I will give you rest" (Matthew 11:28). In His mercy, God will sometimes deal with people for a lifetime, and still they pay very little attention to Him. But what little attention they do give Him, He blesses them in that area.

God is totally motivated by love. We cannot make Him do anything. Trying to force Him to help us by crying about needs He has already met in Christ is outside the realm of His mercy and tenderness. He is waiting for us to walk by faith. Romans 4:16 says: "Therefore it is of faith, that it might be by grace." He wants to deal with us on the basis of grace and mercy. His desire is to bless us even more than we desire to be blessed.

NOTHING YOU CAN DO WILL MAKE HIM LOVE YOU ANY MORE OR ANY LESS. HE LOVES YOU WITH ALL THAT HE IS AND HE IS LOVE.

Even though your body may have been damaged through sin, drugs, alcohol, wrong eating habits, etc., God still compassionately desires to see your body well and strong. His mercy will come in and cleanse you from all unrighteousness. It will replace the sin in your life. Proverbs 16:6 says,

"By mercy and truth iniquity is purged." Or you could say, "By mercy and the Word, iniquity is purged." When mercy flows in, the drug addiction or desire for drink leaves, never to return.

The devil doesn't want you to accept God's mercy. He would like for you to think that one sin calls for another. The truth is that sin calls for the compassion of God, and deliverance and redemption through Jesus Christ. God's mercy is not an excuse to sin. Rather, it is an assurance that we do not have to be entrapped by it. Proverbs 28:13 says, "He that covereth his sins shall not prosper: but whoso confesseth and forsaketh them shall have mercy."

Hope and HEALING

God's mercy provides us with hope. We must have hope for our faith to work because faith is the substance of things hoped for. Without it, our faith has no image to bring to pass.

Lamentations 3:21-23 says, "This I recall to my mind, therefore have I hope. It is of the Lord's mercies that we are not consumed, because his compassions fail not. They are new every morning: great is thy faithfulness."

Our hope is in recalling that the Lord's mercy is renewed every morning. We can place our faith in knowing that God is faithful to His mercy. Every day when we wake up, He is there to fall in love with us all over again!

We are to remind ourselves, as the psalmist did in Psalm 103, of the provisions of God's mercy. The psalmist told his own soul—his own mind—to remember them. He said:

> Bless the Lord, O my soul: and all that is within me, bless his holy name. Bless the Lord…and forget not all his benefits. (Then he went on to list the benefits:) Who forgiveth all thine iniquities; who healeth all thy diseases; who redeemeth thy life from destruction; who crowneth thee with lovingkindness and tender mercies; who satisfieth thy mouth with good things; so that thy youth is renewed like the eagle's.

God causes His mercy to sit as a crown on our heads and to fill our mouths with good things. As we spend time praying in tongues, the Holy Ghost will work on the weaknesses of our flesh and create in us new desires to which our bodies will respond.

God will build within us the desire to pray, walk in love

and speak the right words with the result that we will speak out good things—good prayers and good confessions of faith, mercy and freedom from sin. The filling of our mouth with good things will then, in turn, produce fruit according to the things we have spoken, and our youth will be renewed.

As you meditate on God's mercy, consider these scriptures and see God renewing and changing your life day by day:

- Matthew 9:36; Isaiah 40:11—Jesus has compassion and mercy as the Shepherd of the sheep. He is the Great Shepherd.

- Matthew 15:32—Jesus fed the multitude because of compassion and mercy.

- Mark 6:34—Jesus taught because of compassion.

- Luke 6:36—You are to be merciful as your Father is merciful.

- Luke 7:12-13—Jesus raised the dead because of compassion.

- 2 Corinthians 1:3—Our Father is the Father of all mercy and the God of all comfort.

- Ephesians 2:4—God is rich in mercy.

- Hebrews 4:16—Mercy is obtained at the throne of grace in prayer.

God's mercy is extended toward you. Sin will not keep you from getting healed. The only thing that will keep you from receiving your healing is hanging onto the sin and not repenting of it. James 5:14-15 says: "Is any sick among you? let him call for the elders of the church; and let them pray over him, anointing him with oil in the name of the Lord: And the prayer of faith shall save the sick, and the Lord shall raise him up; and if he have committed sins, they shall be forgiven him."

Pray in faith, but at the same time, be extremely honest with yourself and with God. Stop kidding yourself. If you are living in sin, get it out of your life right now. Make a determination, "I am going to walk holy as my God is holy." The devil will warn you not to make that decision because you might not be able to carry it out, but God sent the Holy Ghost to help you do it in His power. If you do miss it, be honest. Run straight to Him again and call on His mercy that endures forever.

Remember, His mercy is new every morning.

Mercy GIVES GRACE

When the Apostle Paul had a "thorn in his flesh," a messenger sent by Satan to buffet him, he asked God to take it from him three times. (See 2 Corinthians 12:7.) Each time God said, "My grace is sufficient for you." He did not say, "You cannot be delivered" or "My grace is insufficient." He was telling Paul that he was free to receive grace and mercy in that area all the time.

God responded to Moses in much the same way, saying to him, "I am that I am." He was saying to Moses, "When you need credentials while before Pharaoh, that is the I am that I am. I am the water coming out of the rock. I am healing. I am redemption from your sin." In other words, "I am the source of all your need. Whatever you need, I am *that* I am."

Who is God? His identity is summed up in three words—mercy, compassion and love. Through these, He is revealing Himself to us today as He did to Moses. He is saying, "I am Mercy. I am Compassion. I am Love."

THREE

HOW TO HAVE *Faith* IN GOD'S MERCY

Some people have the idea that walking in tune with God means that He will always require them to do without the things they desire—that they can never expect anything good from Him. But this is not true. God's mercy extends to the things we want as well as to our personal needs. He longs to give us more than we could wish for ourselves.

Our ability to ask God for things is not as great as what He yearns to give us. He wants to provide abundance so that we can have plenty for ourselves and plenty to share with others. It is His desire that we align ourselves spiritually with Him, so He can use us as channels to bless others. God knows that prosperity will ruin the one who trusts in his own thinking.

The fool will squander what God has given him on his own lusts and forget that God was the One who gave him power to receive it. So God is waiting for us to get our minds and wills lined up with the mind and will of the Spirit. When our desires match His, He can give to us without having it hurt us.

James 1:4 expresses the will of God concerning us. It says, "But let patience have her perfect work, that ye may be perfect and entire, wanting nothing." It is His desire that we experience no lack in receiving the things we desire. And Psalm 23 reflects this same thought. Verse one says, "The Lord is my shepherd; I shall not want."

As our Shepherd, Jesus has invited us to a banquet table laid out in the presence of the devil and all of hell, where we can feast upon the provisions of His tender mercies. Psalm 23:5-6 says: "Thou preparest a table before me in the presence of mine enemies: thou anointest my head with oil; my cup runneth over. Surely goodness and mercy shall follow me all the days of my life: and I will dwell in the house of the Lord for ever."

Jesus is not talking about the marriage supper of the Lamb or any heavenly feast, because none of our enemies are present in heaven. He is referring to an earthly celebration where we can come and feed on the meat of God's Word at His table. We come to that banquet by an act of our will, by faith. Verse four says: "Yea, though I walk through the valley of the shadow of death, I will fear no evil."

Instead of enjoying the tremendous feast, most people want to get underneath the banquet table and eat the crumbs because they feel so undeserving. God has trouble getting them to receive what He has provided. They forget that although Jesus is the only one worthy of being there, He has extended His mercy to us and paid the price that we might eat with Him.

Remember what Psalm 23 says: "Surely goodness and mercy shall follow me all the days of my life: and I will dwell in the house of the Lord for ever." Can you see what God is saying?

IT IS A SURE THING THAT HIS MERCY AND GOODNESS WILL FOLLOW US.

It is a sure thing that His mercy and goodness will follow us. His mercy is with us through the good and the bad in our lives. And if His mercy is continually following us, then think how easy it is for us to stop and embrace it.

An Act
OF FAITH

God promises us His mercy, but as believers, we must act as though His Word is true, or we will never have any faith in it. You can lay a Bible on the table and say, "Oh, this is a holy book." But if you never depend on what God says in it and act on it, its power will never be released in your life. Holy things are not fragile. You can stand on God's Word when all else looks like it is going to fail.

Realize that you must place your faith in the Word of God for His will to come to pass for you. You must exercise faith in His mercy to receive mercy just as you exerted faith in the law of salvation to get born again. For example, a man could die and go to hell after spending every Sunday of his life in church, if he never placed any action on his belief.

Romans 10:17 says: "…faith cometh by hearing, and hearing by the word of God." Because the Bible is our source of faith, you must hear what the Word of God says about faith in order to develop it. In the same way, if you want to exercise your faith in the mercy of God, you must study and meditate on what the Word of God says concerning His mercy.

Some Christians don't know what they have in the new birth. They have heard the message of the Cross and received faith to be born again, but haven't heard what the Word says about salvation for this life—for today and tomorrow. If they had, they would have discovered that they are already in Christ Jesus, and have received His worthiness to be in the Father's presence. They would begin to understand that God is not looking at them except through eyes of mercy and grace. He sees us in Jesus—in *His* worthiness.

GOD SEES US IN JESUS. HE SEES US IN HIS WORTHINESS.

FOUR

CONFESSION OF *God's* WORD

When I made a decision to live my life based on my place in Jesus Christ, I had to take that place by faith. I couldn't earn it. Jesus of Nazareth hung on a cross and paid for it so I could receive it freely. So when I say, "By His stripes I am healed," I am not just quoting a verse of scripture. It is a statement of where I stand in Him.

If someone were to ask me, "How are you?" I would say, "Great!" even though physically I may feel very sick. I am not talking to you from my place in the natural realm. I am speaking to you based on my position in Jesus Christ. The Word is absolutely true, and I am speaking and acting accordingly. Therefore, I believe what I say comes to pass. I am speaking by faith to exercise that faith and change my physical condition.

I speak to you based on the Word of God, not my physical body. His Word is a higher authority than my body. In doing this, I am putting pressure on the scripture that says, "By His stripes ye were healed" (1 Peter 2:24). I am putting my faith in the Word of God by obeying what Jesus said: "He shall have whatsoever he saith" (Mark 11:23). These scriptures are strong and they will uphold us.

Christians have often misunderstood the confession of faith because it is hard for them to call things that are not as though they were. But the Bible says this is what God does.

One lady I know was rolled up in a ball with muscular dystrophy when her family took her back to the hospital to die. They had to carry her in a sheet because she could not move, but she would not leave the house unless someone would get her shoes. She said, "Go get my shoes or I am not going! When Jesus raises me up, I don't want to walk on those cold hospital floors in my bare feet."

They got her shoes and took her to the hospital. Jesus appeared to that woman in the middle of the night and raised her up. They said when her bones and body straightened out it sounded like somebody shooting a gun in that room.

Developing FAITH IN MERCY

We need to learn to act on what God's Word says and take hold of His mercy like this woman did. We need to learn to place our faith in the mercy of God, especially when we sin. The devil will come along and accuse us, telling us how bad we are for sinning when he is the one that caused us to do it! This is the time to exercise our faith in God's tender mercy.

Second Peter 1:4 says that through His exceeding great and precious promises, we become partakers of His divine nature. His nature is mercy and compassion. We must stand on 1 John 1:9 which says that "If we confess our sins, he (Jesus) is faithful and just to forgive us our sins, and to cleanse us from all unrighteousness."

Don't be moved by feelings of guilt after having acted on God's Word. Stand on it in faith. Stop putting your faith in the way you feel, and begin putting your trust in His tender mercy. Release your faith in His grace and compassion.

Here are four ways to do that:

1. Put the Word first place. Make it the final authority in your life, and change your thinking to agree with it. When the Word says, "If we confess our sins, He is faithful and just to forgive us," begin to have faith in that. Begin to incline your ear to that Word and act on it even when you don't feel like it.

2. Meditate on God's mercy. Keep your mind on Jesus and His mercy. Don't think about all the failure and bad things you've done. If you have never done a good thing in your life, do one before the day is over, and think on it. Remind yourself that God did not get down on you when you were a sinner, and He's not going to get down on you now that you are His child.

You cannot hide your mistakes from God when you fail, but you can see His mercy following you, and you can see yourself yielding to it. Meditate on running to Him when you sin. Then think about this. "How has my life changed since I have believed that His mercy follows me forever? What can I do to stand on the mercy of God?"

Do not meditate on fear. All fear is selfish and is not of love. That makes it a sin. Worry is fear because it is a self-centered concern that always causes you to be afraid of "What's going to happen to me?" The way to cast it out is to replace it with thoughts on love. The Bible says, "…perfect love casteth out fear" (1 John 4:18). The more you meditate on love, the less worried about yourself you will be because you have mercy and goodness following you.

3. Act on the Word. As you meditate on it, the Word will begin casting out fear. As you are released from fear, you will begin to look for opportunities to act on your faith. The more deeply rooted you become in God's Word, the more you will desire for Jesus to bring people across your path so that you can pray for them and see Him raise them up. Remember faith always acts before seeing the results.

4. Make a decision to live the life of love. When we live the life of love, we become vulnerable, but God knows that. The Apostle Paul wrote in Romans 8:36 that to the world we are considered lambs to the slaughter. However, he also said, "…we

are more than conquerors through him that loved us" (verse 37). First Corinthians 13:8 says love never fails. He becomes our shield and protection.

FIVE

THE *Mercy* MINISTRY OF JESUS

T he mercy of God is a celebration of love. In the Hebrew language, mercy, love and compassion all come from the same word, so when you say God is love, you are also saying He is mercy and compassion. We have had the idea that God is just love. God is also *mercy*— the kindness that gives help to the most undeserving. He is also *compassion*—the desire to bear and relieve another's distress.

The combination of mercy, love and compassion form the identity of God Himself. Mercy is not a thing and compassion is not a feeling. Together, they manifest a person. When these three qualities demonstrated themselves in the Son of God, they became a powerful force.

In His ministry, Jesus fully expressed the inner character and nature of His Father each time He acted in mercy. He gave us a revelation that mercy, love and compassion are a person.

Consider these three scriptures as the foundation for studying mercy in Jesus' ministry: Psalm 145:8-9; 2 Corinthians 1:3; Ephesians 2:4.

Psalm 145:8-9 says: "The Lord is gracious, and full of compassion; slow to anger, and of great mercy. The Lord is good to all: and his tender mercies are over all his works." The fact that mercy is over all God's works is important. Mercy, not wrath and power, motivates God to act. It covers every work He performs, and it is the reason He does everything.

> **THE BIBLE NOT ONLY PROCLAIMS THE POWER OF GOD, BUT IT ALSO GIVES US A PICTURE OF HIS MERCY.**

The Bible not only proclaims the power of God, but also gives us a picture—a revelation—of His mercy.

For instance, if you were to compare a father with his

small son, you could easily see which of the two is the stronger. But the only way to get a picture of the love this man has for his son is to see him in action, exercising his power of protection over the child. It is this open display of mercy that allows us to see this father's love.

According to 2 Corinthians 1:3, God is "the Father of our Lord Jesus Christ, the Father of mercies, and the God of all comfort." If you study this verse, you will see what the Spirit of God is saying through the Apostle Paul. He is saying, Jesus Christ is mercy and comfort. Take hold of that. Simply put, mercy and comfort express who Jesus is. God is saying the same thing when He says He is both the Father of Jesus and the Father of mercy and comfort.

The Son of God did not come to judge us or to teach us something through hurt and pain. He came in mercy and comfort to bring us the Father's mercies—salvation, deliverance, healing and more.

Ephesians 2:4-6 says: "But God, who is rich in mercy, for his great love wherewith he loved us, even when we were dead in sins, hath quickened us together with Christ, (by grace ye are saved;) and hath raised us up together, and made us sit together in heavenly places in Christ Jesus."

Together with Christ we were brought to life! Mercy did

it. It made us alive. We can say that "When we were dead in sin, He made us alive together with mercy." Why? Because God is love, and when we say that, we are also saying He is mercy and compassion. Because these words are exact substitutes for one another, we can also say that God "hath raised us up together, and made us sit together in heavenly places in mercy and comfort."

As joint heirs with Jesus Christ, we are able to sit together with Him and partake of His inheritance. This means we share in His ministry of mercy. We become mercy and comfort as He is. In His Name, we have a command to take mercy and comfort to the rest of the world.

If we understand mercy in this light, then we can gain an idea of how great and powerful His mercy is. Too often we have looked at the word mercy like it meant pity or sympathy—a weak thing. The voice of sympathy says, "Oh, I wish there was something we could do." But mercy and compassion use faith and say, "There *is* something we can do. We will pray in the Name of Jesus."

Mercy and compassion act. Nothing is too great for them. Faith works by love and God is love.

The mercy of God is not weak. It was the motivating force behind the plan of redemption that brought Jesus to the earth. In the mind of God, mercy was the revelation that developed the plan. It was God's design to extend His goodwill toward man. Because of mercy, the division between man and God was eternally broken.

When Mary and Joseph were in Bethlehem the night of Jesus' birth, angels came and appeared to the shepherds in the field and proclaimed the glory of God: "Glory to God in the highest, and on earth peace, good will toward men" (Luke 2:14). We have interpreted that to mean goodwill among men. But the Apostle Paul and the Apostle Peter both said that Jesus came preaching peace, not among men, but between God and man. God was proclaiming, "Goodwill to men from God."

MERCY WAS THE MOTIVATING FORCE THAT BROUGHT JESUS TO THE EARTH.

God sent Jesus as a mercy sacrifice to the world. He acted in compassion when He sent Jesus to the cross. Jesus was not the one needing mercy from God. It was you and me. Nevertheless, the Savior came to this world offering His comfort: "Come unto me, all ye that...are heavy laden, and I will give you rest" (Matthew 11:28). And He left this world promising to pray and intercede for us that we might receive the Comforter.

Jesus bore the shame of the cross for the joy of know-ing that we would be able to be reborn in the power and the image of Almighty God and receive the Comforter—the Holy Spirit. He knew we could then manifest the same mercy and comfort on the earth as He had done. "Verily, ver-ily, I say unto you, He that believeth on me, the works that I do shall he do also; and greater works than these shall he do; because I go unto my Father" (John 14:12).

Compassion, mercy and comfort directed all the works of Jesus' ministry. If mercy and compassion were over all the works of God, then it was over all the works of Jesus because Jesus said, "The Son can do nothing of himself, but what he seeth the Father do" (John 5:19). Matthew 9:36 says, "But when he (Jesus) saw the multitudes, he was moved with compassion on them, because they fainted, and were scat-tered abroad, as sheep having no shepherd."

Notice what it says: "He had compassion on them." The word *compassion* means "an inner yearning deep in your bow-els [or innermost being]." It is not just a feeling. It is talking about being led by the Holy Ghost as described in Romans 8:26. He is compassion. There it says that the Holy Spirit will move within us with groanings which cannot be uttered.

SIX

Responding
WITH COMPASSION

Having the Spirit of God move and lead you by compassion from deep within your innermost being is not mental at all. It is beyond feeling and even beyond saying "I feel led." It is where we yearn and experience the heart's desire of God.

From that area, rivers of living water begin to flow. In comparison to a spring of everlasting life which touches only you, a river reaches out to everyone. It flows out of your innermost being for others. Most people have only experienced the spring because they spend the majority of their time praying for themselves and their own needs.

Jesus had a river of life flowing out of Him. He was sensitive to the needs of the people through the Holy Spirit working in Him. The Spirit of God guided Him in the perfect will of the Father. Jesus operated in the gifts of the Spirit to set people free.

From deep within His Spirit, Jesus perceived what the Father would have Him do. He was led by the inward moving and yearning of the Spirit of God: "For what things soever he (God) doeth, these also doeth the Son likewise" (John 5:19).

There were times when Jesus had visions and saw things in His Spirit. On other occasions, the Holy Spirit moved deeply on the inside of Him in the area of knowing, which is the word of knowledge. He perceived what people were thinking or what they had in their hearts. This also happened at the tomb of Lazarus. He groaned from deep within His Spirit, then said to the Father, "I know You have already heard Me."

In a similar manner, we have the capacity to respond to the compassion of God by expressing ourselves through groanings and utterances in the spirit. Sometimes when I pray, it comes out in groanings. I find at times the more I pray the deeper down in my spirit it goes. Sometimes it gets down into an area where it is hard to express in words.

Even Jesus expressed and acted on the inward yearning of compassion. Matthew 9:36 notes Jesus observed that the people were like sheep having no shepherd, and He was moved with compassion on them. His immediate response was to select 12 men to go and minister among them. The choosing of the 12 disciples was directly related to His compassion.

Matthew 10:5-8 says:

These twelve Jesus sent forth, and commanded them, saying, Go not into the way of the Gentiles, and into any city of the Samaritans enter ye not: But go rather to the lost sheep of the house of Israel. And as ye go, preach, saying, The kingdom of heaven is at hand. Heal the sick, cleanse the lepers, raise the dead, cast out devils: freely ye have received, freely give.

Jesus had a revelation of the mercy and comfort of God and this caused Him to want to share it with everyone. He told His disciples to "go preach" and to "heal the sick, cleanse the leper, raise the dead, cast out devils: freely you have received, freely give" (Matthew 10:7-8).

Matthew 9:35 says Jesus went through the cities and villages teaching and preaching. Teaching and preaching are acts of compassion.

When you have the same revelation of God's mercy that Jesus had, compassion will rise up on the inside of you. He was continually praying, at times fasting, always listening to the voice of the Holy Spirit—always walking on the verge of that inner explosion of compassion. We have the same Spirit of compassion living within us, desiring to bring us to that same place of spiritual preparedness, always ready to minister His love and mercy through us.

WHEN YOU HAVE THE SAME REVELATION OF GOD'S MERCY THAT JESUS HAD, COMPASSION WILL RISE UP ON THE INSIDE OF YOU.

In every situation, the compassion of God controlled Jesus. Even in the face of personal tragedy when Herod beheaded His cousin, John the Baptist, Jesus triumphed over His emotions.

Jesus and John had shared a special kinship that began even before they were born. John's mother, Elizabeth, and Mary, the mother of Jesus, spent most of their pregnancies together.

So when Jesus heard of John's death, Matthew 14:13 says that "He departed thence by ship into a desert place apart." Jesus wanted to get out of town away from the people and go to a place to pray. But it says, "When the people had heard thereof, they followed him on foot out of the cities. And Jesus went forth, and saw a great multitude, and was moved with compassion toward them, and he healed their sick."

Even in the face of personal tragedy, compassion moved Jesus to act and meet the needs of the people. After He finished preaching, He called the members of His own staff together to give the people something to eat. He knew that the people were so hungry they would faint if He sent them away. All that was available was a few fish and loaves. Nevertheless, He commanded His disciples to bring the food to Him and instructed the multitude to sit down. In His compassion, He blessed the food, multiplying it so there was more than all of them could eat.

The nature of compassion is to give you a part of what it possesses. This is how it works. For example, in spite of His personal circumstances, Jesus prayed and ministered to the people all day long and then provided for their physical nourishment.

After all this had taken place, it says in Matthew 14:22 that "Straightway Jesus constrained his disciples to get into a ship, and to go before him unto the other side, while he sent the multitudes away." Jesus had a reason in His heart for telling them

THE NATURE OF COMPASSION IS TO GIVE YOU A PART OF WHAT IT POSSESSES.

to go. I am satisfied that the Spirit of God directed Him, in the middle of ministering to the people, to go to the other side of the lake where more ministry awaited Him, more sick, desperate people needing help. Compassion was still directing Him.

He sent the disciples to the other side of the lake and spent the evening in prayer. Matthew 14:23-28 picks up the story: "And when he had sent the multitudes away, he went up into a mountain apart to pray: and when the evening was come, he was there alone. But the ship was now in the midst of the sea, tossed with waves: for the wind was contrary. And in the fourth watch of the night Jesus went unto them, walking on the sea."

His compassion for them brought about this miracle. The Spirit of compassion, the Holy Spirit, revealed they were in trouble. He then enabled Jesus to walk on the water to get to them: "And when the disciples saw him walking on the sea, they were troubled, saying, It is a spirit; and they cried out for fear. But straightway Jesus spake unto them saying, Be of good cheer; it is I; be not afraid. And Peter answered Him and said, Lord, if it be thou, bid me come unto thee on the water."

Because Peter cornered Jesus by saying, "If it be You,"

Jesus could not answer Peter any other way but to say, "Come." Jesus knew Peter did not have the level of faith to walk on that water, but He didn't rebuke him for stepping out on what little faith he had.

Don't ever come against somebody's faith, even if you do not think they are strong enough. Get in there and help them. That is what Jesus did. He was governed by mercy and compassion instead of by legalism, rules and fear. If He had been afraid Peter was going to drown, He would have started sinking Himself.

Peter walked on the water based on the Word of Jesus, "Come." As long as he kept his eyes on Jesus, he made it. But when he started looking at the wind, he became afraid and began to sink.

As he started to sink, Peter cried, "Lord, save me." The Bible says:

> Immediately Jesus stretched forth his hand, and caught him, and said unto him, O thou of little faith, wherefore didst thou doubt? And when they were come into the ship, the wind ceased. Then they that were in the ship came and worshipped him, saying, Of a truth thou art the Son of God. And when they

were gone over, they came into the land of Gennesaret. And when the men of that place had knowledge of him, they sent out into all that country round about, and brought unto him all that were diseased; and besought him that they might only touch the hem of his garment: and as many as touched were made perfectly whole (Matthew 14:31-36).

All this took place because Jesus was moved with compassion out in the desert. In the life of Jesus, compassion took a higher priority than anything else. It caused Him to continually reach out to others and respond to their need. Matthew 20:30-34 is a good example of this:

And, behold, two blind men sitting by the way side, when they heard that Jesus passed by, cried out, saying, Have mercy on us, O Lord, thou son of David. And the multitude rebuked them, because they should hold their peace: but they cried the more, saying, Have mercy on us, O Lord, thou son of David. And Jesus stood still, and called them, and said, What will ye that I shall do unto you? They say unto him, Lord that our eyes may be opened. So Jesus had compassion on them, and touched their eyes: and immediately their eyes received sight, and they followed him.

Jesus had compassion on them, not just for them. The two blind men had caught sight of the fact that mercy would do the job. They cried, "Have mercy," and Jesus was moved with compassion. The power of His mercy was released and brought them their eyesight.

The compassion and mercy of Jesus operated as a force against illness and disease. A good illustration of this is in Mark 1:40-42 when a leper came to Jesus and asked to be made clean. Verse 41 says, "And Jesus, moved with compassion, put forth his hand, and touched him, and saith unto him, I will; be thou clean." As soon as Jesus had spoken, the leprosy immediately departed from him, and he was cleansed.

The Bible does not say, "immediately he was healed." It said that immediately leprosy itself departed, indicating that the spirit life behind the disease left. When that happened, the man's body regained its health. The force that drove the leprosy out was the compassion of God released in the words that Jesus spoke and through His hands.

The mercy of God governed Jesus in every situation. After He healed the leper, Jesus instructed him not to say anything about his healing but to show himself to the priest. However, Mark 1:45 through Mark 2:1 says: "But he went out, and began to publish it much, and to blaze abroad the matter, insomuch that Jesus could no more openly enter into the city, but was without in desert places: and they came to him from every quarter. And again he entered into Capernaum...."

The leper went out and stirred up the countryside to the point where Jesus had to retreat to Capernaum. He called attention to his healing until there were so many people that Jesus could not even minister to all of them. Jesus went to Capernaum. The crowds flooded Him there as they had in the desert. It says in Mark 2:1-4:

> And again he entered into Capernaum after some days; and it was noised that he was in the house. And straightway many were gathered together, insomuch that there was no room to receive them, no, not so much as about the door: and he preached the word unto them. And they come unto him, bringing one sick of the palsy, which was borne of four. And when they could not come nigh unto him for the press, they uncovered the roof where he was: and when they had broken it up, they let down the bed wherein the sick of the palsy lay.

When Jesus saw their faith, He said, "Your sins are forgiven you." What a statement of mercy! He paid no attention
to them taking apart the roof. Through mercy, He saw their
faith. Through mercy and forgiveness, He ministered healing
and deliverance.

SEVEN

Possessing
THE MERCY OF GOD

In most of the religious world, we have
majored in the minors and minored
in the majors. We have majored in God's
anger and minored in His mercy. But
Psalm 30:5 says God's anger "is but for a
moment," *(Amplified Bible, Classic Edition)*
and Psalm 136 says that "God's mercy
endures forever."

There are other areas where we have
gotten the wrong perspective, too. In ma-
joring on the body and minoring on the
spirit, we have placed the wrong emphasis
on the physical realm. The truth is that the
existence of the spirit realm is as real as the

existence of the natural realm. When we were born again, we were born in the spirit. We have tried to get the things of God to go from the outside in, instead of from the inside out. We need to turn inside and let what was born in the spirit flow outward.

Healing is a good example of this. It comes from inside the spirit man out into the body. We have wanted to have healing rubbed on us like an ointment. We have tried to get a treatment by getting into the prayer line expecting to receive healing the way we put on a salve.

Many people have a hard time receiving from God because they approach healing this way. They have had little understanding of the difference between the physical and the spiritual realm. They have failed to understand what Jesus said to Nicodemus in John 3:6: "That which is born of the flesh is flesh; and that which is born of the Spirit is spirit." The flesh represents the natural, or physical realm that is perceived by the five physical senses. By contrast, the spirit realm is more real than what we see, hear, feel and taste.

We must understand that God, a Spirit, created the natural realm. This makes the spirit world, the realm of the Creator, the authority over the natural. Therefore, it would be foolish to consider that the creation is more powerful than the Creator.

When you confessed Jesus as Lord, your spirit was born again. Ephesians 4:24 says you were created in righteousness and true holiness. You are made in the image of God. You are a spirit, you have a soul and you live in a body. To worship God, you must enter the spiritual realm. Jesus said those who worship Him must worship Him "in spirit and in truth" (John 4:24).

Many do not understand that they are a triune being—spirit, soul and body. They have been so conscious of the natural world they have assumed their physical bodies are their true identity, but not so. Our physical bodies are just our earth suits. My coat would be a good illustration of this. I am the life of my coat. When I move, the coat moves. If I were to die, it would be like taking my coat off because dying is simply the laying aside of my natural body.

What I am saying is that we have majored in the minor, which is the natural realm. We get disturbed over what we are going to wear, what we are going to eat and what is going to happen to us. Even preachers have emphasized the minors. They have spent a lot of time preaching to women about what they wear. The Bible says in 1 Peter 3:3-4 that a meek and quiet spirit is important and not the plaiting of hair or the wearing of gold or apparel.

How women dress is a minor point. God is really talking about the spiritual attitude of a woman and whether or not she is trying to call attention to herself through her dress. A woman who has a meek and quiet spirit will come to church to worship God and to help others. She will not come to try and show off her wardrobe.

It is true that some women are dressing to get attention out of pride, but if you major in the spirit, you will settle this matter with God and begin to dress to please Him. Likewise, if you will do the same with mercy and major in it, then the minor of God's wrath will take care of itself. In short, if you will concentrate on the quality of life your spirit is living, you will have no trouble with your body.

I know people who come to meetings where I preach and spend their entire time criticizing what I have on and miss what I say. I am not saying you should not dress well. I think you should represent Jesus Christ in a right way by looking your best with what you have. If you are faithful over little, He will make you master over much. However, we need to put our emphasis in the right places. Many times we have done just the opposite.

Another minor that we have majored in is sacrifice. It seems like everyone has wanted to give up something for

God. God desires mercy rather than sacrifice. Mercy is the major. Mercy is when you give to people out of your heart because you love them and want to see them prosper.

Please do not misunderstand me. Sacrifice is necessary in an obedient Christian's life and needs to be studied. If you will learn mercy while you are learning how to sacrifice, then your sacrifice will count. The Apostle Paul said that even if he gave his body to be burned and gave everything he had to the poor and did not have love, he would gain nothing. So, if you major in the sacrifice without the mercy, it doesn't do any good. You do not impress God.

WHEN YOU GIVE FROM A MERCY MOTIVE, GIVING STARTS FLOWING TOWARD YOU.

When you give from a mercy motive, it starts flowing toward you. As I begin to give, it is given to me again. The more I give, the more I receive and vice versa. It then becomes a continuous cycle of reaching out to others. This is the way mercy works.

Spiritual Answers
VERSUS NATURAL PROBLEMS

The Body of Christ needs to major in mercy. It is what gives us the proper spiritual perspective on the minors. We must see that the problems in the natural, physical realm cannot be solved with just natural realm solutions. It takes a spiritual answer to solve a natural problem.

However, trying to answer a spiritual problem with a natural answer is even more impossible. We cannot get rid of demons with aspirins. That natural answer will not work, yet this is what has been happening in church so frequently. We have gathered committees to take care of spiritual problems and dealt with them in the natural realm. We have asked the person who upsets the church service to leave, instead of getting a prayer group together and interceding for them.

We have attacked cancer the wrong way too. We have approached it as if it were from the natural realm. We have failed to understand that all diseases are not on the same level in the spirit realm. Some infirmities are more natural than others, but cancer is not natural and neither is arthritis or leprosy. Bitterness is their root cause.

Therefore, when it comes to curing cancer and other such spiritual problems, we are not limited to natural means. We can attack the spirit that is causing them with the mercy and compassion of God. In the power of God, we can stand on the Name of Jesus and His redemptive blood. We can take His Word and drive that spirit out.

We must learn not to be governed by the minors in the natural realm. Evangelist Smith Wigglesworth said, "I am not moved by what I feel; I am not moved by what I see; I'm moved by what I believe." And I like to add: "I believe the Word of God, and with the Word of God, I can change the way I feel and what I see." This is the proper perspective.

THE CHURCH HAS BEEN APPROACHING GOD LIKE HE IS *ABLE* TO HEAL THEM, BUT THEY ARE UNSURE HE *WILL* HEAL THEM.

The earthly ministry of Jesus is our example of mercy in operation. His was a ministry of mercy and comfort. He said, "I did not come to destroy the law; I came to fulfill it (Matthew 5:17)." And He did by extending His mercy to us. The Church has not always recognized the mercy of God. They have been approaching God like He is able to heal them, but are unsure that He will.

That would be the same as if your child came to you and said, "Dad, I want to go to college and I know you love me, and I know you would help me if you could. I am just not sure whether you can afford it or not." But if that child said, "Daddy, I want to go to college and I know you can help me, but I don't know whether you will or not." That is an outright insult.

We do not have to approach God either way. We do not have to wonder about His will concerning salvation, healing or prosperity. We already have His will written down in the Word of God for us to know.

Salvation THROUGH MERCY

One of the things God wants us to know is that salvation springs forth from His mercy. Our redemption was conceived, built, carried out and brought into operation from a mind of mercy. A mind of wrath could never have provided redemption. It would have destroyed us and wiped out all mankind, but God was not willing to destroy any of us.

If God had destroyed Satan, according to spiritual law, He would have also destroyed all of Satan's subjects. Death would have flowed from the devil to all who served him. And sadly, the devil is god over a lot of people.

Jesus came down on Satan's level (where we were) in order to bring us redemption from Satan's authority. He had to come down to us. When Adam bowed his knee to an alien spirit, he made Satan his god and gave him his crown. Adam subjected himself to Satan.

Ephesians 2:1-4 says:

And you hath he quickened (or made alive), who were dead in trespasses and sins; wherein in time past ye walked according to the course of this world, according to the prince of the power of the air, the spirit that now worketh in the children of disobedience: among whom also we all had our conversation in times past in the lusts of our flesh, fulfilling the desires of the flesh and of the mind; and were by nature the children of wrath, even as others. But God, who is rich in mercy, for his great love wherewith he loved us, even when we were dead in sins, hath quickened us together with Christ, (by grace ye are saved).

It was out of the love and mercy of God that salvation was born. Then, in Titus 3:3-5 it says:

For we ourselves also were sometimes foolish, disobedient, deceived, serving divers lusts and pleasures, living in malice and envy, hateful, and hating one another. But after that the kindness and love of God our Savior toward man appeared, not by works of righteousness which we have done, but according to his mercy he saved us, by the washing of regeneration and renewing of the Holy Ghost.

The word *love* in this passage is sometimes translated "pity." This is not a good substitute. It should be correctly translated "mercy" as it is in other places. The thought here should be that just as salvation is an act of mercy, so is the Baptism in the Holy Spirit. Jesus came to us as mercy and comfort. He also prayed and asked the Father to send us the Comforter, who has the same ministry of mercy to us that Jesus had.

When a person makes Jesus the Lord of his life, the Holy Spirit changes the nature of the person on the inside. Then, through the work of the Holy Spirit, the outer man begins to be changed. Romans 12:2 tells us we are not to be conformed to the world, but transformed by the renewing of our minds. The Holy Spirit reveals the Word of God to us, and if we are obedient to His Word, our habits and behavior begin to change. The outer man is not changed overnight. The Holy Spirit conforming you to the image of Jesus is a process.

A good illustration of this is the difference between a mule and a racehorse. You can take a mule and raise him in the stable with thoroughbreds. You can give that mule the same food and treatment as a thoroughbred racehorse. You can even do plastic surgery on his ears and make him look pretty good. But when you take him out there to the starting gate and that bell goes off, the mule is a mule and there is no doubt about it. He gets left behind. Why? He is not a mule on the outside, he is a mule on the inside.

God in His mercy knew you could not do anything about the junk on the inside of you. So instead of asking you to clean yourself up, He asked you to receive Him and let *Him* clean you up. It was His mercy that hung on the Cross and sent you the Holy Ghost to be a Comforter to you.

Mercy REPLACES JUDGMENT

Once we have been made new on the inside, we have a responsibility to learn and study and keep ourselves away from the filth. Even when we fall down, if we repent of our sin, God will cleanse us. When we deserve judgment, God gives us mercy. And the Word says in 1 Corinthians 11:31 that if you will judge yourself, you will not be judged. God will judge us in mercy and not with the world. He is merciful to those who judge themselves.

Most of the time, I am harder on myself than He is. In judging ourselves, we need to remember to forgive ourselves and walk in the forgiveness God gives us. The Bible says to love our neighbor as ourselves. If we go overboard in judging ourselves, we are not going to be able to love our neighbor because we will not be able to love ourselves.

God sent mercy and not judgment to us in the form of Jesus. He was born into the world, died on the Cross and was reborn from the dead by the mercy of God.

First Timothy 1:14-15 says: "And the grace of our Lord was exceeding abundant with faith and love which is in

Christ Jesus. This is a faithful saying, and worthy of all accep-
tation, that Christ Jesus came into the world to save sinners;
of whom I am chief."

The Apostle Paul was talking about himself as the chief
of sinners. He meant that salvation was extended to every
human being on the earth through the abundant mercy of
God. The message is true for everyone, and on that basis it is
worthy for them to accept it.

EIGHT

Receiving MERCY

Having mercy available and reaching out to accept it are two different things. Salvation is here for us to take, but we can reject it all day long if we want to. If we do that, the mercy of God will not make any difference in our lives.

It doesn't matter what you have done. Jesus Christ came to save sinners. He did not come for the righteous. There weren't any. The Bible says Jesus died for the ungodly. It is up to you to receive the mercy of God.

Paul wanted to encourage us to take hold of mercy. He was writing to tell us that the great things he experienced did not happen to him because he was an apostle. They occurred because he was a believer. He said, "Howbeit for this cause I obtained mercy, that in me first Jesus Christ might shew forth all longsuffering, for a pattern to them which should hereafter believe on him to life everlasting" (1 Timothy 1:16). Paul became a pattern of the mercy of God for us to follow. Most of us came to the Lord Jesus Christ either directly or indirectly through His ministry because he wrote two-thirds of the New Testament.

The Apostle Peter, like Paul, wanted to direct attention away from himself and the fact that he had walked and talked with Jesus for three and a half years. He wanted people to realize the true basis for his ability to receive mercy and the power to do miracles. When he healed a lame man, he said to the people who were around, "Why look ye so earnestly on us, as though by our own power or holiness we had made this man to walk" (Acts 3:12). In other words, he was saying, "It was neither our holiness nor our calling, but faith in the Name of Jesus that made this man strong."

I once knew a quiet, elderly man who was head usher in a church. His name was Brother Steel. One day he was a few minutes late coming to church. I found out he had been fishing that afternoon and had been bitten by a water moccasin. He pulled up his pant leg and showed me where the snake had bitten him. I asked him what he did. He said, "I reached down there and got him and said, 'I'll tell you one thing old boy, in the Name of Jesus the Bible said if a snake bites you, he ain't going to hurt you. There ain't no way you're going to hurt me.' And I just throwed him away." He said, "I didn't feel too good. That's kind of the reason I was late to church."

This man just believed the Bible. Like Paul, he obtained mercy because without the mercy of God there is not anyone who can reach down and get a cottonmouth water moccasin by the hand, curse it in the Name of Jesus and throw it away. This man did what the Bible commands us to do, and that is to have faith in the Name of Jesus.

We must first obtain mercy before we can pattern ourselves after Paul. When Paul was born again, the mercy of God got down on the inside of him and brought forth a revelation that I could see. His testimony is a witness to God's mercy. In the Bible, we see him first as a killer. Then we see him as a preacher of the gospel. As a preacher, he was beaten with rods, lashed with 40 stripes three times, thrown into dungeons and shipwrecked twice. He experienced perils from countrymen and fought wild beasts—all to get the Word of God to people and set them free.

A Spiritual FORCE

From Paul we can see that mercy is not only the pattern we are to follow, but a spiritual force. At the new birth, the Holy Spirit imparts to us what the *King James* Bible calls "everlasting life." In Greek, it is called *"zoe* life" or the life of God. *Zoe* is the element that makes God, God. It is eternal because you cannot kill or stop it.

Jesus said, "I have come that they might have *zoe* and have it in abundance" (John 10:10). We are forever as God is forever, because we have the substance of *zoe* life within us.

Receiving everlasting life is not the same thing as living forever. You were created a spirit and a spirit can never cease to exist. To a spirit, death is being separated from the life of God. You will exist forever whether you serve the devil or whether you serve God.

In the second resurrection, the graves will give up the

bodies of every person who has died without the Son of God. Those who have died without obtaining God's everlasting life will manifest for eternity the presence of sickness, disease and death just as they did in their physical life.

When someone loses his soul, he loses control of it. A person who goes into hell does not go blank. He has a better memory and consciousness than he had when he was in his body. Look at the rich man in Luke 16 who died and went into hell. He lifted up his eyes and said, "Father Abraham." Not only did he recognize Abraham, but he knew his brothers and Lazarus the beggar. He said, "Send Lazarus down here with water to put on my tongue (v. 23-24)." He was wiser in the spirit after he died than he was before.

One time God opened my eyes and allowed me to see what people's spirits looked like when they were not attached to their physical bodies. I saw good Christian people with undeveloped spirits that looked awful. They had great big heads because they were mentally developed and little, spindly, scrawny, spiritual bodies caused by a lack of spiritual food. These people had fed on religion, the junk food of the spiritual realm. It had ruined their bodies.

If a boxer can work for months and months to get in a ring for 15 rounds, what should a believer be able to do for Jesus to gain a crown of glory? All Christians have tremendous potential within them. The zoe life of God in their spirits contains a unique substance the Bible calls "the fruit of the spirit." This fruit contains nine parts: love, joy, peace, long-suffering, gentleness, goodness, faith, meekness and temperance.

The Bible considers these qualities a fruit because it continually grows and produces. But it can also be compared to an explosive, for it only releases its tremendous power when ignited.

WE DO NOT IGNORE THE NEGATIVE CIRCUMSTANCES WHEN WE SPEAK HIS WORD. WE JUST DO NOT LIVE IN THEM.

For example, the Bible says that *faith* will move mountains and cast things into the sea. But we can carry faith around with us forever and never move a mountain. To see the power of faith, it must be ignited like a stick of dynamite. The fuse that sets off this power is the spoken Word of the living God.

This does not mean that we ignore the negative circumstances when we speak His Word. It means we do not live in them. We are deciding by what we say, the kind of forces we release. We can either release the forces of the kingdom of hell with all its demons or the forces of the kingdom of

God with all its angelic army. Both sides are standing, waiting to see what we will say. In one sense, we are like kings holding court.

Because we are made in the likeness of Jesus, our words hold authority, as His do. Our words are the determining factor. What we say is what we get.

Igniting
MERCY'S POWER

The words we speak are important. Holding onto our confession of the living Word will ignite the mercy of God! Hebrews 4:12-14 says:

> For the word of God is quick, and powerful, and sharper than any twoedged sword, piercing even to the dividing asunder of soul and spirit, and of the joints and marrow, and is a discerner of the thoughts and intents of the heart. Neither is there any creature that is not manifest in his sight: but all things are naked and opened unto the eyes of him with whom we have to do. Seeing then that we have a greater

high priest, that is passed into the heavens, Jesus the Son of God, let us hold fast our profession.

We are to keep a faithful confession based on the Word of God. We can do that because our High Priest has already been touched with the "feelings of our infirmities" and "was in all points tempted like as we are, yet without sin" (Hebrews 4:15). On that basis, we are to come boldly to the throne of grace and as verse 16 says "obtain mercy" through the mercy of our High Priest, Jesus.

IF WE CLING TO CONFESSIONS OF HOW BAD WE FEEL AND DO NOT TAKE HOLD OF MERCY, WE ARE NOT IGNITING THE DYNAMITE.

If we cling to confessions of how bad we feel and do not take hold of mercy, we are not igniting the dynamite. We are igniting some other force that we did not want to blow. The wrong words give the devil power he does not rightfully possess. It is like holding an explosive and giving him the match. When we confess sickness and disease, we let him blow us away with our own guns.

The spiritual law of the Word of God is in Mark 11:23 where Jesus said: "That whosoever shall say unto this mountain, Be thou removed, and be thou cast into the sea; and shall not doubt in his heart, but shall believe that those things which he saith shall come to pass; he shall have whatsoever he saith."

That law works on the negative side, as well as the positive side. If Satan had any power, he wouldn't have to use deception. He would just kill us. But, since he is powerless, the only thing he can do is deceive us by lying to us. He tries to work and put us into an area where we will make the wrong confession. If he can get us to say, "I'm so bored. I'm so nogood. Oh, I'll never make it. Oh God, I'm so sick and tired," he knows we can have whatever we say.

NINE

Receiving
FAITHFULNESS

If we are having trouble keeping our confession of faith, we need to take hold of mercy. Obtaining mercy will enable us to be faithful to God. Paul illustrated this in 1 Corinthians 7:25. In dealing with family affairs in the Church, he said, "Now concerning virgins I have no commandment of the Lord: yet I give my judgment, as one that hath obtained mercy of the Lord to be faithful."

It was the revelation of mercy that caused Paul to be faithful to God. It was as if he said, "I've never received a commandment of God in this, but I am faithful enough to God and He is faithful enough to me that I know how He thinks about it, and I will just go ahead and tell you." Paul knew that obtaining the mercy of God would keep men from fainting and preserve their faith.

The Apostle Peter acknowledged the scriptural truth of what Paul said and continued the same thought when he wrote 2 Corinthians 4:1: "Therefore seeing we have this ministry, as we have received mercy, we faint not; but have renounced the hidden things of dishonesty, not walking in craftiness, nor handling the word of God deceitfully; but by manifestation of the truth...."

Have you ever fainted in the middle of your confession of faith and said, "Dear God, I just can't hold on to this any longer. I don't think I can continue to stand up. I have been confessing this thing for weeks and weeks. How long am I going to have to do it?" If you have come to that place, re-member Ephesians 6:13 says, "Wherefore take unto you the whole armour of God, that ye may be able to withstand in the evil day, and having done all, to stand. Stand therefore...." If you are ready to stand forever, you won't be there very long.

Joshua and Caleb held onto their confession of, "We can take the land" for 40 years, until they were both 80 years old. Then Caleb said to Joshua, who was their spiritual leader,

"Give me that mountain. I can take the land." His confession had remained unchanged.

Caleb knew of the faithfulness and mercy of God. It motivated him to draw closer to God instead of running from Him. He was convinced his God was able. When we get a revelation of mercy and obtain it for ourselves we will begin to speak it out in faith. That's when mercy begins to explode and manifest itself outwardly.

It all comes down to this: God's original plan was for man to live in close communion with Him. But after Adam sinned, this was no longer possible. God could only deal with man at arm's length. Fellowship was impossible.

But, the Father had mercy on man and sent His only Son to be our Savior and Redeemer. Through His death and resurrection, Jesus restored us to our rightful place in God's original plan—a place of fellowship and communion with the Father.

As joint heirs through Christ's saving power, we have the right to God's mercy and all that goes with it. So, take advantage of this gift from God. Ignite the power of mercy in your life by spending time in

AS JOINT HEIRS THROUGH CHRIST'S SAVING POWER, WE HAVE THE RIGHT TO GOD'S MERCY AND ALL THAT GOES WITH IT.

prayer and fellowship with the Father. Study His Word. Take hold of the promises found in His Word, and by faith speak your needs into being. Confess and believe in His power. If you do these things, God's mercy will continually be manifest in your life. For His mercy endureth...*forever!*

Prayer for Salvation and Baptism in the Holy Spirit

Heavenly Father, I come to You in the Name of Jesus. Your Word says, "Whosoever shall call on the name of the Lord shall be saved" (Acts 2:21). I am calling on You. I pray and ask Jesus to come into my heart and be Lord over my life according to Romans 10:9-10: "If thou shalt confess with thy mouth the Lord Jesus, and shalt believe in thine heart that God hath raised him from the dead, thou shalt be saved. For with the heart man believeth unto righteousness; and with the mouth confession is made unto salvation." I do that now. I confess that Jesus is Lord, and I believe in my heart that God raised Him from the dead. I repent of sin. I renounce it. I renounce the devil and everything he stands for. Jesus is my Lord.

I am now reborn! I am a Christian—a child of Almighty God! I am saved! You also said in Your Word, "If ye then, being evil, know how to give good gifts unto your children: HOW MUCH MORE shall your heavenly Father give the Holy Spirit to them that ask him?" (Luke 11:13). I'm also asking You to fill me with the Holy Spirit. Holy Spirit, rise up within me as I praise God. I fully expect to speak with other tongues as You give me the utterance (Acts 2:4). In Jesus' Name. Amen!

Begin to praise God for filling you with the Holy Spirit. Speak those words and syllables you receive—not in your own language, but the language given to you by the Holy Spirit. You have to use your own voice. God will not force you to speak. Don't be concerned with how it sounds. It is a heavenly language!

Continue with the blessing God has given you and pray in the spirit every day.

You are a born-again, Spirit-filled believer. You'll never be the same!

Find a good church that boldly preaches God's Word and obeys it. Become part of a church family who will love and care for you as you love and care for them.

We need to be connected to each other. It increases our strength in God. It's God's plan for us.

Make it a habit to watch the Believer's Voice of Victory Network television broadcast and become a doer of the Word, who is blessed in his doing (James 1:22-25).

About the Author

Kenneth Copeland is co-founder and president of Kenneth Copeland Ministries in Fort Worth, Texas, and best-selling author of books that include *Honor—Walking in Honesty, Truth and Integrity,* and *THE BLESSING of The LORD Makes Rich and He Adds No Sorrow With It.*

Since 1967, Kenneth has been a minister of the gospel of Christ and teacher of God's WORD. He is also the artist on award-winning albums such as his Grammy-nominated *Only the Redeemed, In His Presence, He Is Jehovah, Just a Closer Walk* and *Big Band Gospel.* He also co-stars as the character Wichita Slim in the children's adventure videos *The Gunslinger, Covenant Rider* and the movie *The Treasure of Eagle Mountain,* and as Daniel Lyon in the Commander Kellie and the Superkids™ videos *Armor of Light* and *Judgment: The Trial of Commander Kellie.* Kenneth also co-stars as a Hispanic godfather in the 2009 and 2016 movies *The Rally* and *The Rally 2: Breaking the Curse.*

With the help of offices and staff in the United States, Canada, England, Australia, South Africa, Ukraine and Latin America Kenneth is fulfilling his vision to boldly preach the uncompromised WORD of God from the top of this world, to the bottom, and all the way around. His ministry reaches millions of people worldwide through daily and Sunday TV broadcasts, magazines, teaching audios and videos, conventions and campaigns, and the World Wide Web.

Learn more about Kenneth Copeland Ministries by visiting our website at **kcm.org.**

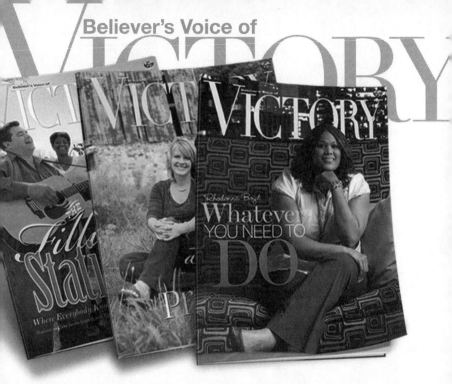

When The LORD first spoke to Kenneth and Gloria Copeland about starting the *Believer's Voice of Victory* magazine...

He said: *This is your seed. Give it to everyone who ever responds to your ministry, and don't ever allow anyone to pay for a subscription!*

For more than 50 years, it has been the joy of Kenneth Copeland Ministries to bring the good news to believers. Readers enjoy teaching from ministers who write from lives of living contact with God, and testimonies from believers experiencing victory through God's Word in their everyday lives.

Today, the *BVOV* magazine is mailed monthly, bringing encouragement and blessing to believers around the world. Many even use it as a ministry tool, passing it on to others who desire to know Jesus and grow in their faith!

**Request your FREE subscription to the
Believer's Voice of Victory magazine today!**

Go to **freevictory.com** to subscribe online, or call us at
1-800-600-7395 (U.S. only) or **+1-817-852-6000.**

e're Here for You!®

ur growth in God's Word and your victory in Jesus are at the very center of r hearts. In every way God has equipped us, we will help you deal with the ues facing you, so you can be the **victorious overcomer** He has planned for 1 to be.

e mission of Kenneth Copeland Ministries is about all of us growing d going together. Our prayer is that you will take full advantage of all The)RD has given us to share with you.

herever you are in the world, you can watch the *Believer's Voice of Victory*)adcast on television (check your local listings), kcm.org and digital streaming ,ices like Roku®. You can also watch the broadcast as well as programs from zens of ministers you can trust on our 24/7 faith network—Victory Channel®. sit govictory.com for show listings and all the ways to watch.

ir website, **kcm.org,** gives you access to every resource we've developed your victory. And, you can find contact information for our international ices in Africa, Australia, Canada, Europe, Ukraine, Latin America and our adquarters in the United States.

ch office is staffed with devoted men and women, ready to serve and pray with 1. You can contact the worldwide office nearest you for assistance, and you can l us for prayer at our U.S. number, +1-817-852-6000, every day of the week!

e encourage you to connect with us often and let us be part of your ryday walk of faith!

us Is LORD!

Kenneth & Gloria Copeland

nneth and Gloria Copeland